VIKING
Published by the Penguin Group
Penguin Books USA Inc., 375 Hudson Street, New York, New York 10014, U.S.A.
Penguin Books Ltd, 27 Wrights Lane, London W8 5TZ, England
Penguin Books Australia Ltd, Ringwood, Victoria, Australia
Penguin Books Canada Ltd, 10 Alcorn Avenue, Toronto, Ontario, Canada M4V 3B2
Penguin Books (N.Z.) Ltd, 182–190 Wairau Road, Auckland 10, New Zealand

Penguin Books Ltd, Registered Offices: Harmondsworth, Middlesex, England

First published in 1997 by Viking, a division of Penguin Books USA Inc.

1 3 5 7 9 10 8 6 4 2

Collection copyright © Harriet Ziefert, 1997
Illustrations copyright © Emily Bolam, 1997
All rights reserved

Library of Congress Catalog Card Number: 96-61796
ISBN 0-670-87569-4

Manufactured in China
Set in Meridien

MOTHER GOOSE
MATH

Selected by Harriet Ziefert
Illustrated by Emily Bolam

Viking

Chook, chook, chook, chook, chook,
Good morning, Mrs. Hen.
How many chickens have you got?
Madam, I've got ten.

Four of them are yellow,
And four of them are brown,
And two of them are speckled red,
The nicest in the town.

One, two, three, four, five,
Once I caught a fish alive.
Six, seven, eight, nine, ten,
Then I let it go again.

Why did you let it go?
Because it bit my finger so.
Which finger did it bite?
The little finger on the right.

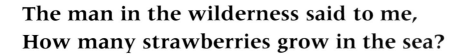

The man in the wilderness said to me,
How many strawberries grow in the sea?

I answered him, as I thought good,
As many red herrings as swim in the wood.

Five little monkeys walked along the shore;

One sailed away and then there were four.

Four little monkeys
climbed up a tree;

One of them fell down—

Then there were three.

Three little monkeys

found a pot of glue;

One got stuck in it—

Then there were two.

Two little monkeys found a currant bun;

One ran away with it—
Then there was one.

One little monkey cried all afternoon,

So they put him in an airplane
And sent him to the moon.

I bought a dozen new-laid eggs
Of good old Farmer Dickens;

I hobbled home upon two legs
And found them full of chickens.

Three young rats with black felt hats,
Three young ducks with white straw flats,
Three young dogs with curling tails,
Three young cats with demi-veils

Went out to walk with three young pigs
In satin vests and sorrel wigs.

But suddenly it chanced to rain
And so they all went home again.

Sing a song of sixpence,
A pocket full of rye;
Four and twenty blackbirds
Baked in a pie.

When the pie was opened,
The birds began to sing;
Was not that a dainty dish
To set before a king?

The king was in his counting house
Counting out his money;
The queen was in the parlor
Eating bread and honey.

The maid was in the garden
Hanging out the clothes,
When down came a blackbird
And pecked off her nose.

An apple a day
Keeps the doctor away.

Apple in the morning,
Doctor's warning.

Eat an apple going to bed,
Knock the doctor on the head.

Three each day, seven days a week,
Ruddy apple, ruddy cheek.

Hickety, pickety, my black hen,
She lays eggs for gentlemen;
Gentlemen come every day
To see what my black hen does lay;
Sometimes nine and sometimes ten,
Hickety, pickety, my black hen.

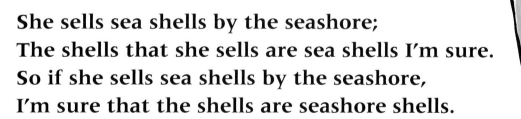

She sells sea shells by the seashore;
The shells that she sells are sea shells I'm sure.
So if she sells sea shells by the seashore,
I'm sure that the shells are seashore shells.

1...2...
Buckle my shoe;

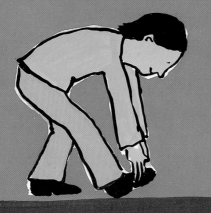

3...4...
Knock at the door;

5...6...
Pick up sticks;

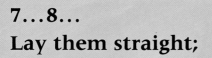

7...8...
Lay them straight;

9...10...
A big fat hen;

As I was going to St. Ives,
I met a man with seven wives.
Every wife had seven sacks;
Every sack had seven cats;
Every cat had seven kits:

Kits, cats, sacks, and wives,
How many were going to St. Ives?